T0380894

TIME FOR 'GUN' TROL

AJOYKUMAR VASUDEVAN

To order additional copies of this book, contact:
Xlibris
844-714-8691
www.Xlibris.com
Orders@Xlibris.com

ISBN: Softcover   978-1-6698-3619-3
         EBook   978-1-6698-3618-6

Print information available on the last page

Rev. date: 07/05/2022

Dedication

To thousands of innocent little kids and people who lost their lives in the brutal shootings happened at various schools and public places in United States.

Acknowledgement

My sincere thanks to my mother Saroja Vasudevan for her whole hearted prayers in bringing this guide, Mahalakshmi Sanga Pillai and C.M. Joseph who took much initiative in the production of this guide with their reviews and feedbacks. And my sincere thanks to Bhuvaneswari Venkatesh for her yoga drawings.

Preface

Mass shootings on school children and in public places are a regular feature and not just rare incidents in America. The deaths of students, teachers, and security personnel during such firings are continuously on the rise.

How much pain would have been felt by those small children, dying because of firing inside their schools, and how much more pain lingers in the hearts of unfortunate parents?

How much blood has been shed in the US soil due to such incidents?

Where are those young buds now? All their dreams of blooming have been shattered.

I am praying for those thousands and thousands of small souls and innocent people to rest in peace in Heaven.

Oh God. Please don't allow such terrible things to happen again. Please bless our children to grow with good health and a good mind. Please bless them to grow with glittering happiness as good citizens.

Please bless our children to enjoy living on this soil, as we elders enjoy.

The Purpose of Writing this Guide

Whenever a gun shooting occurs and dozens of people killed, we light candles and pray for the departed souls to rest in peace.

The very next day we are busy with our work and will forget all the miseries that had happened.

Again, somewhere in America, the gun shootings will happen somewhere and the same candle lights and prayers are repeated.

How many times you will repeat these last rites with tears?

My intention is not to blame anybody. We cannot change anything that has happened in the past.

My prime focus is to stop these types of barbaric acts in future.

How?

We will see the strategies in the following pages.

I came here from a developing country, India. United States has given freedom, comforts, luxuries and even financial assistance when I was sick. I am always grateful to this country. As a token of gratitude want to do something constructive to the problem of mass shootings in America.

Hence this guide.

Gun Shootings in Schools and Public Places

It is believed that on an average one firing takes place every week in a school/public place.

One day my car had issues and I called the towing service. An aged American gentleman came to tow the car. I was travelling in his truck. He asked me from which country I was.

I said South India.

Then he asked me whether I like America.

I said happily that I like America and the freedom and comforts I enjoy here.

Then the aged gentleman told me in a sad feeling the following words.

"I don't like my country America."

I was shocked to hear this.

I said "Are you joking?"

He replied in a firm voice. "No friend, our country is not a safe place to live. Everyday there is a gun shooting somewhere. How can you lead a peaceful retired life here? I want to go to some other country for my retirement."

I have talked to several people after that and most people reflected this idea.

It is with pain and sufferings I am writing these lines.

America is a great country. Americans are smart and strong people. We have no doubt that America is a super, powerful Nation.

When the mighty American Government takes action to eradicate the terrorists' activities all over the world, why is it not taking effective steps to eradicate these kind of mass shootings at schools/public places in their country itself, which is no doubt a domestic terrorist activity.

Instead of taking temporary measures of solving the problem, why are no actions being taken to eradicate such activities entirely? Is it not our duty as Americans to eradicate such firing incidents???

Why is there a hesitation? What are the hurdles??

Wikipedia has given statistical details of firings held at school and details of victims etc., from 1840 to date.

If you see the list of school shootings and mass shootings in U.S, your heart will stop working for few seconds.

The dreams of parents are shattered. The children coming to school with books and dreams are also shattered because of some cruel minded student who got a rifle in his hand.

Upon seeing these firings and deaths, I am also shattered in heart and mind like all other parents.

I have lost my only daughter due to a brain tumour at her prime age of 17 years. So, I know the pain and suffering which were undergone by those parents who have lost their children in such firings. Even after 10 years, I could not control the pain of my daughter's death.

I am an addict of singing movie songs "incorrectly". So, when I did such things at home, my daughter whenever would witness such nonsense, used to give me a whack on my back and advise me to sing correctly.

When memories of my daughter are flashing, I cannot control my tears. Whenever I read or hear of children's sufferings of any kind, I immediately recollect my memories of my daughter and tears are spontaneous. This pain will be with me till my death.

Such is the power of affection towards children and their love.

My deepest condolences to the parents of the deceased children.

Why Such Firings are Taken Place at Schools and Public Places in United States

First and basic reason is the failure in arriving strong and right gun reforms.

Yes, the politicians and social reformers tried in the past but in vain. So, is it knowledgeable to drop this effort once for all?

Secondly, people sell rifles at black markets/online, without checking the background of those who are purchasing and other details.

This carelessness ultimately results in loss of many human lives.

Furthermore, AR-15 type rifles are largely in use in America. Approximately 8 million rifles are in use in the United States.

Even though the rifle manufacturers argue that these AR-15 type rifles are being used only for hunting and gaming, they are also used for firing on human lives. Advantages of using this type of rifle are its light weight and accuracy on the target. I am not interested in investigating this rifle, but we have to look for the consequences of using this kind of weapon freely in the hands of people in America.

Though Americans are high intellectuals and brilliant in all attitude, it is surprising to know that they have not taken necessary steps to completely eradicate such firing activities carried out by mentally sick people against school children, teachers and innocent public.

Thirdly parents. Yes, this is true. Some parents are careless in keeping these dangerous weapons safely and out of reach.

Their children are able to steal the rifles from their parents and use them.

This is the pathetic situation prevailing in the country.

My intention is not to criticize the matter, but to eradicate the firings once for all from America.

My intention is to inform - how to totally stop these incidents???

This is a very big social problem.

We are here to take steps to help the future generation to live happily and peacefully in this country. So, it becomes our social and moral responsibility to take up this subject with sincerity and with social consciousness.

Request to Honourable President Joe Biden and U.S Lawmakers:

As you all know that this kind of firings have been going on for the past 180 years, please take up this matter as a WARTIME crisis.

We know that the U.S Government and politicians tried to make necessary gun reforms in the past but they failed to arrive at suitable solutions.

Recently our honourable president Joe Biden had signed the gun reform bill into law. This is really a welcome measure and expected by the American people for decades.

However, we have to take more steps to stop this brutal gun shootings once for all from this land.

I want to reiterate that only Government can change this situation.

I assure this GUN REFORMS CAN BE DONE by you definitely.

Here are some guidelines to do this:

1. "Right to keep gun for self-protection" is our freedom and in the constitution.

   Pistols can alone do the role of self-protection. Why do we need semi-automatic weapons in the name of self-protection?

   When we look back the past incidents, mass shootings are done with the help of semi-automatic weapons.

   A law can be immediately imposed to keep pistols alone for self-protection and the semi-automatic weapons kept by the people should be surrendered immediately to the nearest Police station.

2. A license should be given to keep the pistols for self-protection.

3. The age to keep pistols for self-protection should be raised to 23.

4. Those who have fire arms without license and those who do not abide these reforms should be prisoned and fined with huge penalties.

5. Gun sales in online/black market must be prohibited and treated as illegal and those who do so will be punished severely with life imprisonment and penalties.

6. A team with social reformers can be formed to study and implement the necessary gun reforms.

7. This Team can go to Australia and Germany to learn how those countries succeeded in implementing strict measures for gun reform.

Here I am bound to say that our American people have the self-pride about their intelligence. The Americans want to be leaders and not followers. Self-pride will not go useless if you follow the best practices around us.

In 1996, Australian Government took strong and stringent steps on the holdings and usage of rifles by their citizens when a firing was occurred with semi-automatic rifle and death toll was around 35.

In 2016, Sydney University took up research and released an article in the JOURNAL OF THE AMERICAN MEDICAL ASSOCIATION.

In the 18 years preceding 1996, Australia experienced 13 fatal mass shootings in which 104 victims were killed and at least another 52 were wounded.

There have been no fatal mass shootings since that time (after 1996), with the study defining only one mass shooting as having at least five victims.

In October 2017, there was a shooting at Las Vegas (America) where 59 people were found dead due to the barbaric incident. Australian External Minster Ms. Julie Bishop has given an Interview after the incident, wherein she has informed preventive steps taken by their country through their legislature.

Strict gun reforms are made in Germany too.

Do we oppose the crimes made against the innocent people of America or are we going to compromise the term "freedom"?

We must be careful in distinguishing the words FREEDOM and RESPONSIBILITY.

8. There should be capital punishment for any carelessness of the people (even if they are parents of the murderer) in losing the rifles or bullets, or for misusing the rifles by their children. As per reports, it seems that the rifles are stolen from parents and used in most of the shootings at schools.

9. Teachers in schools must be allowed to carry pistols with them. This will create a fear among the sick minded student to carry out mass shooting in schools.

Steps to be Taken by Department of Education, School Authorities and Parents

School authorities:

A lot of initiatives are taken at the schools.

Metal detectors, bullet proof doors and windows, secret cameras, additional securities, training and other precautionary measures are being implemented in a lot of schools.

Steps are taken to alert through Public Microphone systems system when some suspicious people are inside the campus.

Training is given to schools to take shelter and find escape routes during such firings.

Despite such precautionary steps, firings and deaths are still continued.

We have to thank and appreciate the preventive steps already taken by school administration.

However some more actions are needed from Department of Education and Schools:

As said by LAO TZU "The journey of a thousand miles begins with one step."

Yes. **We need a very big social reformation.**

Firstly, we have to educate our children about the value of doing YOGA exercises. By doing Yoga exercises, it is reported both scientifically and medically that yoga helps to have good attitudes of mind and body of the children. When doing yoga, children are:

(a) benefited physically,

(b) purifying their mind from external distractions and children are doing well in their studies,

(c) getting self-motivation and some unnecessary doubts and fears are gone,

(d) less susceptible to disease,

(e) of good health of both body and mind

(f) creative and helpful to society.

All schools may be directed to carry out YOGA exercise compulsorily on daily basis to their children, at least for 30 minutes daily.

Every knowledgeable person knows that YOGA is not a RELIGIOUS ACTIVITY and in fact it is a way of life to achieve healthy mind and body.

So why should we hesitate to adopt such BEST PRACTICES?

I strongly recommend the Department of Education and School authorities to train each and every child with the help of a yoga instructor.

The Physical Education Teachers can get training from the yoga instructors and thus Physical Education Teachers can be able to teach our children in schools.

Some basic and important yoga exercises are given below for reference.

Standing posture:

1. Tadasana

2. Utkatasana

3. Trikonasana

4. Padahasthasana

Sitting Posture:

5. Padmasana

6. Virasana

7. Navasana

8. Pachimottasana

Backward Posture

9. Bhujangasana

10. Dhanurasana

11. Ustrasana

Inverse Posture:

12. Halasana

13. Sarvangasana

Relaxation

14. Savasana

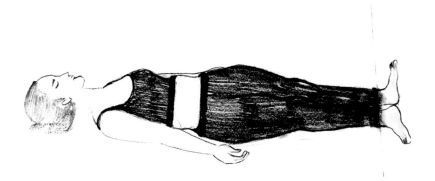

Secondly, a 30 minutes class should be devoted for the teaching of Moral subject everyday to all the students.

Syllabus and curriculum may be designed to include Moral studies accordingly by the school administration.

It is a good thing that unlike other countries, in America, schools are given freedom to design a syllabus of their own.

Thirdly, schools should show to their students, biography movies/documentaries of famous leaders, scientists and sports personalities, so as to create a positive change in the minds of young students.

Fourthly, it seems a flaw in the opening of doors inside schools with individual ID. Whenever a student uses his/her ID to open the door, there is a gap and it takes few seconds to close the door again. Others behind him/her also can enter into the building using this gap and without using their ID.

A person or a student with a bad intention can also use this loop hole and can enter into the building without much effort. To minimize this danger, students should be educated to not let strangers enter with them. All visitors should be directed to the front desk, through the main entrance.

Responsibilities of Teachers

Whenever there is a doubt on the behaviour of a student, teachers should report the matter to school administration immediately. As per reports, in some of the cases, teachers have failed to take preventative action as soon as they hear about the suspicious behaviour of the students involved in the incidents at the initial level.

If actions are taken at the root level by giving counselling to the children, then there is lot of possibilities to change and bring them to the main stream of a harmonious life.

The dedication given by the teachers in their job is a remarkable thing.

Teachers are the ladders and having a very big social responsibility in uplifting the student life.

It is true to say 'Teachers are God's servants'.

My humble and best wishes for the dedication of the teachers.

Responsibilities of Parents

A society consists of a bunch of unique individuals.

If people decided upon a harmonious society, then each person should have a social responsibility in developing their family in a healthy atmosphere and with accountability.

If each and every family does this social responsibility with care and concern, then the society will flourish better.

Parents have the big responsibility in bringing their children into the harmonious society.

1. Prayer habit: -

As soon as kids wake up in the morning, we should cultivate the habit of praying according to their faith. Kids should be asked to wake up and do a quick prayer even before going to the rest room.

"Oh God, let us thank you for giving this day to us. (Everyday billions of people go to bed and among them millions of people do not wake up the next morning. bear this in mind)

Oh God, let us thank you for making us happy. (Count your blessings)

Oh God, please bless us with your kindness

Oh God, please help us to come out of darkness,

please make us disciplined with good health and sound mind.

please give us good education and compassion on others.

please make us fit to do services to our parents, teachers, neighbours and to the country!"

After Prayers, kids may be allowed to carry out their morning duties. You may have a doubt about such early morning prayer and that too before going to restroom.

The early morning hours are so precious and so important.

If kids are having tension in the morning, then they would be spending the whole day with tension.

If they are in the habit of doing prayer as soon as they are out of the bed, then they get a balanced mind to counter the everyday challenges. By this prayer, positive vibration will be always around them.

By saying thanks to God, He will protect us from evils and help us to be harmonious and happy. Parents and kids should create a habit of doing prayer wherever and whenever they get time. By saying thanks to the God, your life will be so blessed and will be harmonious.

This is a "secret of happiness".

2. Train children to drink water:

After the children returned from the rest room, train them to drink good plain water of at least 500 ml in the empty stomach. It will clean their stomach and give numerous health benefits.

3. Train the children to breath correctly:

Most of us do not know how to breathe.

Yes. This is a fact.

It is an essential practice but we are careless in this important aspect.

Train the children to breathe correctly. They must inhale clean air to the full lungs capacity and exhale all the air inhaled correctly every time. This can be done at least 21 times a day.

This practice is good for the lungs and can avoid lungs related diseases in future.

4. Food habits: -

A scientific research study conducted about "food and behaviour among children", it was reported that there is a direct and proportionate connection between the food and attitudes of the mind.

Fast food, Junk food, sugar filled drinks are spoiling the physical health and mental health of the children, so parents should carefully avoid providing such foods to their children.

Vegetables, milk products, fruit juices, and other products which are considered to be harmonious to health, can be given to children.

5. Sleep: -

Eight hours of sleep is needed for all growing children. The complete rest for eight hours helps them to wake up fresh the next morning and gives a lot of stamina for the whole day. Children should be asked to avoid using cell phones. As per reports, use of a cell phone for long hours creates neck pain, hearing problems, brain diseases, retinal diseases and more.

6. Games: -

Playing outdoor games under the supervision of parents helps children a lot. It creates self-confidence, courage, team spirit and is good for health. Outdoor games help the children to sleep well at night and clears the fear and doubts in their minds and provides them with good personality.

7. Spend more time with Children: -

An idle mind is a devil's workshop. So never allow your children to be alone. Create a reading habit in them and help them to do little tasks, games, etc., at home. Spend time and make them comfortable and happy because of your presence.

Love your children. It is true to say that those kids who had love and affection from their parents will not indulge in cruel activities.

8. Provide Financial assistance: -

It is in the culture of America that after children are of age do part time work in order to continue their higher studies.

If we see this at a Macro level, it seems to be good for the children to stand on their own without troubling their parents.

The real truth is that there is a lot of stress on the children who are doing part time work for the need of taking up their higher studies.

No Organization will give you a fair wage or salary without extracting a lot of work from you. Even in the part time work, the time of work and the volume of work seems to be beyond normal. And students are young and they have the stamina to do such strenuous work. They earn well in such jobs.

But the bad part is they get the tendency to spend the money on unhealthy and unnecessary entertainment.

They are unable to spend enough time for their studies. In some cases, they forget their higher education.

As per research ultimately in 43% of college students say they have stopped their meals in order to afford course materials. If this report is true, then it will be a horrible thing to know the health condition of such children.

When health condition is not good, how will they have a balanced and good mind?

Without good health of the body and mind, how will these children lead a good society in future?

What is going to happen to America with these ill health children?

Parents/Government should provide financial assistance to complete education of their children for a suitable career in the future.

9. Man is not an island: -

A man or woman cannot live alone and away from the society.

A man or woman cannot be an island in what he/she believes. Roman 14.7 and Ezekiel Chapter 2:1 – 10 tells the same.

Teach children to be cordial with others and love all beings.

Good relationship with parents, brothers, sisters, teachers, co-students is important to build up a strong positive personality of the child.

10. Tolerance and love towards other religions:

Please train the children not to show hatred towards other religions. Instead train them to be cordial and kind towards other religious people. This is very important and will shape the child's personality as an optimistic human being in this competitive world.

Finally

We are living in a world, where we are not realizing the pain of death, unless it is happening to us in our family. We become ignorant of others' pain and death.

We have seen in "Animal Planet" channel that some buffalos saved elephant calf from the lions. We praise such brave acts done by the animals.

But when we witness some firing incident that happened at school or college, we just feel pity for a few seconds and then move on to our daily lives.

Why is there no social responsibility within us to make a protest on such incidents?

This is the exact time for awakening.

This is the biggest social problem before us.

And I know that reforms can't be made within a day or two.

But I am also sure and hopeful to see a bright future among our children when these recommended changes are implemented at all level.

There is no gain without pain.

I love America equally to my beloved country India.

I am not asking to change your cultural heritage or your customs. I want to see implementation of the reforms recommended in this guide in order to enrich our children's future. I am hopeful that the future generation will be with good health and sound mind. And America will prove its supremacy "again" with the good healthy generation.

Wishing best of luck for all people living in America!!!

With full of love and affection to the children of America!!!

About the Author

He has a Master's degree in Commerce and more than 23 years of experience in finance in corporate sector and 7 years in the development sector.

He enthusiastically remembers his involvement in working with the people affected by HIV/AIDS, Tsunami of 2004 happened in South India and for Water and Sanitation in the remote poor villages of Bihar in North India.

Printed in the United States
by Baker & Taylor Publisher Services